SPELLED
OUT

Contentment Spelled Out

Published by Know The Truth
P.O. Box 30250
Anaheim, CA 92809-0208
(888) 644-8811

ISBN 978-1-7360801-2-2

Cover and interior design by 2 Creative Houstons, 2creativehoustons.com

Published in the United States by Know The Truth, Anaheim, California.

SPELLED OUT

PHILIP DE COURCY

CONTENTS

FLEEING

DISCONTENTMENT

D_2 I_1 S_1 C_3 O_1 N_1 T_1 E_1 N_1 T_1 M_3 E_1 N_1 T_1

FLEEING DISCONTENTMENT

You have probably heard of these two categories of people: the haves and the have-nots. For our purposes I would like to add a third and fourth category: the have-to-haves and the have-to-have-what-the-haves-have. Wanting more than what you have, wanting what others have, and even wanting others not to have what they have are serious temptations for each of us. We are tempted because apart from a work of God's grace, we have hearts that are concaved, turned on themselves, as Martin Luther described. Our hearts naturally put our own wants, desires, and pleasures ahead of everything else. As they say, the heart wants what it wants.

It is also a serious trap because the world is constantly telling us that we need more. Consumerism and consumption are the Western way. Having it all is the American Dream. No matter how wealthy we are or how much we possess, Wall Street and Madison Avenue will tell us it is not enough. Our culture feeds us the salt of discontentment, which in turn creates a covetous thirst for things. We live in a society marked by "inextinguishable discontent," as Bible teacher Gary Inrig notes. He says, "We have been trained by the hidden persuaders in our society that we need to acquire, consume, upgrade, and enlarge. In such a context, the concept of 'enough' is rare. No one is advertising the virtues of contentment.

But the Holy Spirit uses just that word to put His finger on one of the most significant and sensitive issues in our lives."[1]

Think about how easy it is to slip into discontentment. You sit down on the sofa for a relaxing afternoon catching up on some magazines. You learn that you need a Peloton exercise bike if you want to achieve optimal fitness. Suddenly, your gym membership doesn't look like it's going to cut it anymore. You flip the page and discover that real men drive Ford F-150 trucks. It makes you second-guess the sensible minivan you bought last year to transport your family of six.

You look at the next magazine, but it only makes you feel worse because it sends you the message that you need that well-tailored suit and designer loafers to look like a million bucks. Your own wardrobe starts to feel a bit drab. Once you've finished flipping through those magazines, you are downright depressed. Nothing you have is good enough, new enough, or fancy enough.

You see, contentment is not a matter of how much you possess but a matter of perspective. It is a heart issue. It is having what I like to call "soul sufficiency." One man might build a Fortune 500 company and remain unsatisfied, greedy for more. Another man might not know where his next meal is coming from yet still be at peace within his soul because he is trusting God. The point is, true contentment from God is an inward state of joy, calm, and rest that is not tied to external circumstances or things.

Contentment does not come instantly or instinctively to us. It must be learned. In Philippians 4:11–12, the Apostle Paul lends us insight into this: "I have learned in whatever state I am, to be content: I know how to be abased, and I know how to abound. Everywhere and in all things I have learned both to be full and to be hungry, both to abound and to suffer need."

Isn't it good news that contentment is attainable for everyone? Paul says twice here that he has learned it. He has acquired it over time, mastering it through the various circumstances he's gone through. It's important to note that Paul uses two different words for "learned" in this passage. The first one, in verse 11, is a general term for the acquisition of knowledge. The second word, however, in verse 12, is a unique word that means to be initiated into the mysteries of something. Think of it as being inducted into a secret society or cracking a code to gain access to a hidden chamber. That is the word Paul is using, and I think it is purposeful. He is saying, "In every situation or season, God has me in a certain chamber to learn certain lessons. And, when I learn something more about my own deficiency and God's sufficiency, He grants me access to the next chamber. I'm going to have to learn greater detachment from material possessions, worldly desires, and the things I've made idols of. I'm going to have to discover the greatness of God's love and the astounding wealth that is mine in Christ." It is by no means easy, but as we persevere through these challenges that He appoints for us, we will develop contentment.

Before we get into the particulars of contentment, it is worthwhile to grasp the seriousness of discontentment before a holy God. Living in a perpetual state of want may be the norm in society, but it saddens and angers the Lord. Remember when the Israelites were grumbling in the wilderness on the journey to the promised land? God had delivered them from slavery in Egypt, guided them with His very presence, and provided food from heaven, yet they were fixated on what they lacked. They made God so angry that He sent a fire to the outskirts of the camp that killed some of them (Num 11:1–3). May we not make light of something so offensive to God. Let's take the time to see discontentment and its offspring—covetousness—as God sees it.

BEWARE OF COVETOUSNESS

Covetousness is an *inordinate* longing or craving, a dominating selfish desire for something belonging to another (Josh 7:21; Mic 2:2). It is a consuming preoccupation with worldly things not in our possession (Luke 12:15). Covetousness is desire inflamed and running a fever. And it is a particular brand of discontentment that we need to fight against.

Covetousness is a sin (Exod 20:17). We are forbidden from coveting other people's property or possessions. Harboring discontentment in our hearts, pining over our neighbor's progress and prosperity, and defining life by the pursuit and possession of things are all prohibited by the tenth commandment: Do not covet. The sin of coveting is also a form of idolatry. It is no mistake that this is the command that closes out the Ten Commandments. Coveting keeps you from loving God and neighbor, which is the whole law (Matt 22:37–40). Coveting is idolatry because it exalts created things above the Creator (Rom 1:25). It says, "I *must* have (fill in the blank)." It makes a god out of your belly (Phil 3:19). It says that God and His gifts are not enough.

However, here is a disclaimer: not all desire is wrong. God made us creatures of desire. Aspiring to have something more or to be something more is not unbiblical (Deut 8:18; 1 Cor 12:31; 1 Tim 3:1). But ask yourself: Is what I desire morally acceptable?

Does it suit me, and can I reasonably attain it? Are my motives clean, pure, and kingdom-based? If the answer is no, your desire may be crossing the line into covetousness.

CONSEQUENCES OF COVETING

For our purposes, I will use the words "covet" and "envy" interchangeably. Although there is a distinction, they are twins belonging to the same family of sinful desires. Covetousness breeds and gives birth to envy. And they both have serious and grave consequences. Proverbs 27:4 says, "Wrath is cruel and anger a torrent, But who is able to stand before jealousy?" Envy is more powerful and destructive than anger. According to Proverbs 14:30, "A sound heart is life to the body, But envy is rottenness to the bones." It is like a cancer, eating away at your life and vitality. Let's look at some specific implications of covetousness.

IT DISHONORS

Covetousness dishonors God. I've already noted that it makes us lawbreakers and idolaters. It also is an insult to God and His character. If you covet something you don't have—which God hasn't given you either because it's forbidden or because of His mysterious providence—you are, by implication, questioning God's wisdom. You are chafing at God's provision. When you compare your situation to your neighbor's situation, you can begin to doubt God's goodness and fairness.

It seems Peter experienced this kind of dissatisfaction and doubt when Jesus told him how he would be martyred (John 21:18–23). Upon hearing the news, Peter looked over to John and said something to the effect of, "What about him? I'm not sure I like what I heard, so tell me something about him. Is his end as bad as mine? That'll make me feel a little bit better. I want John to suffer if I'm going to suffer." What did Jesus say to Peter in response? "Well, what's that to you? This is My will for you. You've got your assignment."

When we are covetous, we often start competing with others. We buy into the lie: *I deserve better than him.* We may think our problem is with other people, but our problem is with God because we are ultimately questioning His sovereignty when we want something more than what He has given at the time. It grieves Him that we believe we need something outside of Him to be satisfied. We are denying the promise that we have all we need for life and happiness in Him (Ps 16:11; 23:1; 1 Pet 1:3). Covetousness drills holes in that theology.

The Greek word for contentment literally means "sufficient." Biblical contentment means having a clear sense of your sufficiency as a child of God. Think about who you are *in Christ*—a sinner saved by grace, declared righteous, adopted into God's family, given the gift and gifts of the Holy Spirit, loaded down with great and exceeding promises in the gospel, and bound for a glorious eternity in the presence of God, where there are pleasures forevermore. Meditate on that reality and let it fill you with its richness. God has freely given you His love, presence, and friendship (Rom 8:31–39). Is it not more than enough to conclude that you are sufficiently taken care of? I love how the Puritan pastor Jeremiah Burroughs paraphrases Paul's words in Philippians 4:11–13: "I find a sufficiency of satisfaction in my own heart, through the grace of Christ that is in me. Though I have not outward comforts and worldly conveniences to supply my necessities, yet I have a sufficient portion between Christ and my soul abundantly to satisfy me in every condition."[2]

IT DEPRECIATES

Covetousness cheapens life, reducing it down from a glorious pursuit of intimacy with the Creator to a tawdry accumulation of created things. We are invited to spend our days enjoying the friendship of God (Isa 41:8). What a lofty privilege it is to get up every morning and say, "Father in heaven, You are glorious. Today I will honor Your Name in what I do. I want to be a means of bringing Your kingdom and rule to bear upon this earth. Please be kind to supply my needs and keep me from evil" (see Matt 6:9–13). We have been called to a grand pursuit. But covetousness shrivels our purpose down to the stockpiling of stuff that will rot and rust (Matt 6:19–20).

Jesus makes this point in Luke 12: watch out for covetousness, because your life should not be defined by your wardrobe, bank account, or the car you drive. If you do happen to have a nice home in a good neighborhood and drive a fancy car, give God the glory and use those blessings to serve others. But don't let those things be what gets you up in the morning.

Covetousness switches the price tags in life, inflating the value of earthly things and deflating the value of eternal things. This is why Paul warns the rich not to trust in riches, which are unreliable (1 Tim 6:6–10). You came into this world with nothing, and there will be no U-Hauls behind the hearse when you leave this world.

The United States is one of the richest nations on earth, yet its citizens are some of the unhappiest people on earth. We could learn a lesson or two from those in less privileged places. I remember meeting a special little girl when I was ministering in Zambia some years ago. We had the kids design their own T-shirts. I'll never forget this girl—dirt poor, no shoes on her feet. You know what she painted on her T-shirt? "Life is good." She may have had a mud hut for a home, but she had the maturity to know that happiness comes from within and life is not about what you have. I think she understood that God owned her. *Life is good because I am God's child.*

I often say that the cure for being tempted by the pleasure of sin is not simply prohibition, but it is finding a greater pleasure in Christ.

Similarly, the cure for covetousness is not merely prohibition, although it is a starting point, but a greater coveting—a hunger for God. We find many examples in the Psalms of this right kind of covetous desire:

- *The law of the Lord is perfect, converting the soul . . .*
  More to be desired are they than gold,
  Yea, than much fine gold;
  Sweeter also than honey and the honeycomb. (Ps 19:7–10)
- *One thing I have desired of the Lord,*
  That will I seek:
  That I may dwell in the house of the Lord
  All the days of my life,
  To behold the beauty of the Lord,
  And to inquire in His temple. (Ps 27:4)
- *Whom have I in heaven but You?*
  And there is none upon earth that I desire besides You.
  My flesh and my heart fail;
  But God is the strength of my heart and my portion forever.
  (Ps 73:25–26)

In The *Weight of Glory*, C. S. Lewis points out that the problem is not that our desires are too strong but that they are too weak.

> Indeed, if we consider the unblushing promises of reward and the staggering nature of the rewards promised in the Gospels, it would seem that Our Lord finds our desires not too strong, but too weak. We are half-hearted creatures, fooling about with drink and sex and ambition when infinite joy is offered us, like an ignorant child who wants to go on making mud pies in a slum because he cannot imagine what is meant by the offer of a holiday at the sea. We are far too easily pleased.[3]

That is the right diagnosis. God examines us and determines that our coveting isn't too strong; it is, in fact, not strong enough. We settle for the world's table scraps when we could be feasting at the King's banquet as guests of honor (Ps 23:5; Song 2:4).

IT DEPRESSES

Coveting things that you think will make you happy actually just breeds unhappiness. What's more, it can make you sad at the happiness of others and incapable of celebrating their successes. It makes you the downer at the party! Covetousness makes you sour because it breeds ingratitude, questions providence, takes spiritual riches for granted, and makes you self-absorbed. It does not multiply joy or foster peace.

The life of King Saul is a sobering picture of how covetousness depresses. In 1 Samuel 18, David returns home from several military victories. His troops have enjoyed great triumphs over the Philistines. As David returns, the women come out onto the streets singing, "'Saul has slain his thousands, and David his ten thousands'" (v. 7). Here is what we read in verse 8: "Then Saul was very angry, and the saying displeased him." He was not happy. He was sullen. He was embittered and jealous of David, wanting the greater praise and attention. Verse 9 says, "So Saul eyed David from that day forward." He gave David the evil eye, so to speak, because of the envy boiling within him and its fruits: displeasure, hatred, and suspicion.

We find another example of how envy gets you down in King Ahab (1 Kings 21). Naboth the Jezreelite owned a vineyard next door to the king's palace. King Ahab eyed it one day and thought it would make a beautiful vegetable garden for his palace. He asked Naboth if he could buy it, telling him to name his price. Naboth replied that it's not for sale. (Sidenote: If King Ahab had read his Bible, he would have known you are not allowed to sell the inheritance God has given to your family.) Notice how Ahab reacts to Naboth's answer: "So Ahab went into his house sullen and displeased because of the word which Naboth the Jezreelite had spoken to him. . . . And he lay down on his bed, and turned away his face, and would eat no food" (v. 4). He's acting like a moody teenager! He lies in bed and sulks, staring at the wall, talking to nobody. His breakfast lies cold on the bedroom floor because his disappointment has swallowed him in sadness.

Unlike some other sins, covetousness is no fun. Let's be clear that I'm not commending any sin. Rather, I am saying that while some sins afford momentary pleasure, covetousness is a wretched experience from start to finish. Its cravings are never satisfied, leading to a life of perpetual upset and self-torment.

IT DESTROYS

The sin of coveting leaves a trail of destruction it its wake (Prov 27:4). It dissolves contentment, splits churches, separates friends, and blows up marriages. It creates havoc in the home and injects hostility into the office. It can lead to lying, theft, violence, and even murder.

Paul describes the damage it can do in 1 Timothy 6, which I referenced earlier. Let's look at this passage carefully: "But those who desire to be rich fall into temptation and a snare, and into many foolish and harmful lusts"—now notice this—"which drown men in destruction and perdition" (v. 9). The NIV says these lusts "plunge people into ruin." The Greek word for "drown" or "plunge" is a nautical term. It is the same word used in the story of when the disciples were out fishing in Luke 5. They were fishing all night but caught nothing. (I can relate. The only thing I ever caught fishing in the Irish Sea was the cold.) As they returned, Jesus told them to put their nets down one more time. They complied, and they were blessed with a catch so big that the boat began to sink. They called over another boat to take some of the fish off their hands, but then both boats were overwhelmed and began to sink. There's our word—plunging, sinking, capsizing. That's how Paul describes what covetousness does to people. It drowns them in sorrow and discontentment.

Think about how Joseph was impacted by the envy of his brothers in Genesis 37. Jacob favored Joseph over his brothers and gave him a special coat of many colors to make it official. It stoked the sibling rivalry. Joseph further fueled the fire when he told his brothers about his dream: I will rise above you, and you will bow down to me. His brothers hated him, and in their fierce jealousy, they wanted to kill him and conspired to get rid of him for good (vv.18–23). Not only did they betray their brother, but they also broke their father's heart and crushed his spirit (vv. 28, 34). Envy truly is a green-eyed monster that wants to destroy everything in its path.

Let's not be blind to the deadly dangers of this sin. There is an old story passed down in Jewish tradition about a shop owner who received a visit from an angel. The angel offered to grant the man one wish for anything he wanted. But the angel would grant the wish on one condition: he would also grant the man's rival—whom he deeply envied—a double portion of what the man wished for. The man immediately knew what to ask for: to be blind in one eye.

Sin will always take you further than you want to go, keep you longer than you want to stay, and cost you more than you want to pay. The wages of covetousness are steep (Rom 6:23).

FINDING

CONTENTMENT

C_3
O_1
N_1
T_1
E_1
N_1
T_1
M_3
E_1
N_1
T_1

FINDING
CONTENTMENT

By now we have seen that covetousness is no small thing. It can escalate into chaos and all kinds of evil (Gen 37:11; Acts 7:9; Jas 3:16): conspiracy (Gen 37:18), mockery (Gen 37:19), murderous intentions (Gen 37:20), violence (Gen 37:23), cruelty (Gen 37:24), betrayal (Gen 37:26–28), lies (Gen 37:32), and great harm to others (Gen 37:34). Left unchecked, it can fester and ooze the bile of bitterness in our lives.

You might call covetousness the "if only" syndrome. If only I were married. If only I had a bit more money. If only I lived in a larger home. If only I didn't have this type of body or this health problem. If only it were that simple! But it isn't. Contentment will not come when you get what you want. Contentment is an inward condition, not an outward one. It is the result of spiritual discipline, not material wealth or physical blessings. Wishing for something more or something else may seem harmless, but it can easily put you in a miserable place of always feeling robbed. While focusing on what is missing in your life, you can miss out on much of life itself. You need a shift in perspective.

Consider the lifelong effects of the "if only" syndrome:

> It was Spring, but it was Summer I wanted:
> The warm days and the great outdoors.

It was Summer, but it was Fall I wanted:
The colorful leaves and the cool, dry air.

It was Fall, but it was Winter I wanted:
The beautiful snow and the joy of the holiday season.

It was Winter, but it was the Spring I wanted:
The warmth and blossoming of nature.

I was a child, and it was adulthood I wanted:
The freedom and the respect.

I was 20, but it was 30 I wanted:
To be mature and sophisticated.

I was middle-aged, but it was 20 I wanted:
The youth and the free spirit.

I was retired, but it was middle-aged I wanted:
The presence of mind without limitations.

My life was over,
and I never got what I wanted.[4]

Everyday temptations to discontentment lie all around us, like land mines waiting to be tripped if we are not spiritually alert and grounded in Christ. In the battle against covetousness, the best defense is a good offense. That is why a proactive pursuit of contentment is essential for the healthy believer.

J. C. Ryle, the faithful Protestant pastor and bishop of Liverpool, said, "Two things are said to be very rare sights in the world—one is a young man that is humble, and the other is an old man that is content."[5] So let's seek to learn contentment. It is a spiritual discipline that will take a lifetime to master. But we have the hope and promise that God will work in us to form it as we put in the effort to flesh it out in our lives (Phil 2:12–13; 4:13).

I want to be clear that biblical contentment is not complacency. It is not a passive acceptance of where you are at in life. Before Paul talks about contentment in Philippians 4, he describes a certain kind of discontentment that should mark believers:

> Not that I have already attained [perfect knowledge of Christ], or am already perfected; but I press on, that I may lay hold of that for which Christ Jesus has also laid hold of me. Brethren, I do not count myself to have apprehended; but one thing I do, forgetting those things which are behind and reaching forward to those things which are ahead, I press toward the goal for the prize of the upward call of God in Christ Jesus. (Phil 3:12–14)

Paul is expressing here that because he is not yet all that Christ wants him to be, he is always striving to become more than he is. He is modeling for us a necessary dissatisfaction with our own holiness and nearness to Christ that should motivate us to excel still more. He wants us to embrace greater change. He wants us to always be stretching forward, straining to become the righteous saints we were redeemed to be (Ps 63:8). This kind of discontentment pleases the Lord. I like to say that we need to be discontented contented people: discontent with who we are but content with what we have and where God has us for the moment.

In his book *The Art of Divine Contentment*, the Puritan preacher Thomas Watson tells us *not* to be content with three things, the first being with your natural state.[6] In other words, don't be content with remaining who you are *apart* from Jesus Christ, because Scripture says you are enslaved to sin. You are born a rebel with a bent toward disobedience. Do not remain in that state. If you are still in Adam, you need to be in Christ. Repent of your sin and flee from the wrath of God. See and embrace the love of God, which was demonstrated in Jesus' death on the cross for you. Don't be content with your natural state (Eph 2:1–10).

Secondly, Watson says not to be content in any situation that dishonors the Lord.[7] So, the unsaved need to get saved, and the saved need to stop living lives of disobedience. If you claim to be a believer but know that something you are doing or pursuing is outside of the will of God, stop, turn around, and come home. Life will not go well for you until you repent of your sin and obey His Word (Ps 32; Ps 51). If life happens to be going well on the wayward path, you can be sure that it will only be for a season.

Finally, Watson advises the believer not to be content with little grace (John 1:16; Jam 4:8).[8] That is the message of Philippians 3. Don't be complacent about where you are at in your walk with Christ. He didn't save you just to give you a "get out of jail free" card. He saved you to transform your character and way of life after the glory of God and the beauty of Christ (Rom 8:28–30). So don't settle for little grace. Strive to lay hold of that for which Christ laid hold of you (Phil 3:12).

True contentment is a gift from God, available to every believer who learns how to receive it. It is that blessed inward state of acceptance and trust that will carry you through the highs and lows of life. In the remainder of this book, we will look at biblical principles for cultivating contentment. Because I want these principles to be a helpful guide to contentment that you can easily remember, I have outlined them using the word CONTENT as an acrostic:

C: Cherish Christ
O: Offer thanks
N: Nurture love
T: Tithe, and then some
E: Embrace providence
N: Nix ungodly desires for more
T: Take the long view

I pray that this will be a road map for you to become a person marked by deep and unshakeable contentment in God.

CHERISH CHRIST

No matter where life finds a Christian, life finds the Christian in Christ. As God's children, we can have a fixed faith on fixed things amidst changing circumstances. Even the hardest of times need not beat us down or turn us into victims of chance. I love what pastor and Bible teacher Warren Wiersbe says: "We cannot control or change the world around us, but we can control the world within us. It has often been said that what life does to us depends on what life finds in us."[9] We can handle the blows of life because we have the strength of Christ, our solid Rock, dwelling within. He continually pours His sustaining power into us to handle the next setback, sickness, and sorrow.

The heart of contentment is an abiding soul sufficiency that is rooted in a growing relationship with Christ. Paul had a strong sense of contentment that came from his intimate connection to the Lord: "Not that I speak in regard to need, for I have learned in whatever state I am, to be content: I know how to be abased, and I know how to abound. Everywhere and in all things I have learned both to be full and to be hungry, both to abound and to suffer need. I can do all things through Christ who strengthens me" (Phil 4:11–13).

Paul's words and conviction are more extraordinary when we remember that Paul was writing them while under house arrest (Acts 28). His life was hanging in the balance. His foes were taking advantage of his imprisonment to discredit him and get an edge in ministry (Phil

1:15–18). But he was able to find contentment in this bleak situation because his contentment was internal, not external. His happiness and well-being were not tied to his circumstances. He was not more content when he was full and less content when he was empty. You may have heard the saying that just as a cloudy day shouldn't rob us of contentment, a sunny day shouldn't supply it either. That's a good statement.

In the Greek, the terms "to be abased" and "to abound" in Philippians 4:12 are used to describe the ocean tide that ebbs and flows. So, Paul is essentially saying, "As the tide comes in and goes out, God's blessing comes in and goes out. Health comes in; health goes out. But I'm happy either way because my contentment is within me." And the secret sauce in Paul's contentment was the indwelling Christ (Gal 2:20; Col 1:26–27). He had a continual infusion of strength from Christ, of which there is an inexhaustible supply.

You, too, have the fountain of Christ within you (John 7:37–39). Whatever circumstance you are in, He is pouring strength into you. Sufficient grace is given to you for every new day. Our cup overflows in Christ (Ps 23:5). You simply need to bring your cup and put it under the fountain, and He will fill it with new peace, hope, and perseverance. To change the metaphor, He is the vine, and we are the branches. If we abide in the vine, we will thrive, blossom, and bear fruit (John 15:1–5). Practically speaking, if you are living in daily communion with Christ and drawing upon the means of grace—prayer and fasting, reading the Word, and fellowship with the saints—you will be connected to a continual supply of His supernatural strength and help.

Paul's contentment was not stoicism or human willpower. Don't abuse Philippians 4:13. Have you ever seen athletes wearing those bandanas that say, "I can do all things through Christ who strengthens me"? Don't think you are going to suddenly miraculously bench-press 200 pounds because you can do all things through Christ. It is foolish to think, "I'm not going to study for my exam because I can do all things through Christ who strengthens me." That is not what this verse means. When the 200-pound barbell falls on your chest, or you fail the exam, it will be your fault because you have taken Philippians 4:13 out of context. The "all things" of verse 13 are the "all circumstances" of verses 11 and 12. Christ gives us the strength to live the "all things" that God has sent our way.

Paul had the assurance of "always having all sufficiency in all things" with God (2 Cor 9:8). We find this same confidence in the Old Testament, in saints such as King David. In Psalm 23, he made the bold statement that he lacked nothing because God was with him: "The Lord is my shepherd; I shall not want" (v. 1). The title "Lord" refers to the covenant name of God: Yahweh. He is the Self-Existent One—the One who depends on no one and the One upon whom everyone depends (Acts 17:22–31). He existed in self-sufficiency before creation, and He needs nothing outside of Himself to be Himself. Because David's shepherd is Yahweh, he lives with the assurance that he has all he needs. He lacks nothing in both easy times and hard, in both green pastures and grim valleys. Author Paul Powell puts it like this:

> For our weariness, there are green pastures;
> For our anxieties, there is still water;
> For our falterings, there is restoration;
> For our perplexities, there is guidance;
> For our fears, there is comfort;
> For our enemies, there is a feast;
> For our hurts, there is anointing;
> For the end, there is the Father's house.[10]

I once heard R. C. Sproul say, "God doesn't need me to be me for Him to be Him, but I need Him to be Him for me to be me." That is the kind of sufficiency we are describing. There is no "want" in God, so if I am in Him, I also have no want. That is the point I want to drive home. In fact, the Greek word for "contentment," *autarkēs*, actually means "sufficient." So, contentment is a mindset of having enough no matter what situation you are in.

I appreciate Warren Wiersbe's perspective on contentment. He says, "Contentment, then, is actually *containment*—having the spiritual resources within to face life courageously and handle it successfully.

Contentment is divine adequacy. Contentment is having that spiritual artesian well within so that you don't have to run to the broken cisterns of the world to get what you need. The power of Christ in the inner man is all we need for the demands of life."[11] You can tell yourself this: "Because I am in union with Christ, I am contained; I have all the resources that I need within me for life and godliness. I am intimately connected to the ultimate source of life and have a strong sense of inner abundance." We find this understanding of divine adequacy in the words of the psalmist: "Whom have I in heaven but You? And there is none upon earth that I desire besides You. My flesh and my heart fail; But God is the strength of my heart and my portion forever" (Ps 73:25–26). We can withstand anything because in Christ we have everything.

Nothing can get us down because we are seated with Christ in the heavens. In his letter to the Ephesians, Paul extols the spiritual riches and resources believers have been given access to in Christ. We have "every spiritual blessing in the heavenly places" (1:3). We were chosen "before the foundation of the world" (1:4). We were adopted by the Father as sons (1:5). We are "accepted in the Beloved" (1:6). We are redeemed and forgiven of our sins by the "riches of His grace" (1:7). We have an eternal inheritance and are "sealed with the Holy Spirit" as a guarantee of it (1:11–14). God gives all believers these resources from the day they are saved, and that is why Paul prays that they might fully understand the vast riches they already possess in Christ (1:16–19).

It reminds me of the story of Danny Simpson:

> If Danny Simpson had known more about guns, he might not have needed to rob the bank. But in 1990, in Ottawa, Canada, this 24-year-old went to jail, and his gun went to a museum. He was arrested for robbing a bank of $6,000 and then sent to jail for six years. He had used a .45 caliber Colt semiautomatic, which turned out to be an antique made by the Ross Rifle Company, Quebec City, in 1918.
>
> The pistol is worth up to $100,000—much more than Danny Simpson had stolen. If he had just known what

he carried in his hand, he wouldn't have robbed the bank. In other words, Danny already had what he needed.[12]

If Danny Simpson had known what he had, he might not have felt so poor and driven to desperation! Know that you have everything you need and more in Christ. Cut out the bellyaching. You have a peace that can't be destroyed, a joy that can't be suppressed, a love that can't be abated, a grace that can't be arrested, a strength that can't be exhausted, a comfort that can't be lessened, a hope that can't be disappointed, a glory that can't be diminished. Treasure and cherish Christ, in whom we have these priceless resources.

O

OFFER THANKS

Contentment grows in the soil of gratitude. You can't be content with what you have if you don't appreciate what you have, and you won't appreciate what you have unless you take the time to account for what you have. Practicing gratitude and thanksgiving is a means of grace. As you take inventory of God's many gifts to you—both spiritual and tangible—you declare God's goodness and experience a deepening sense of contentment (Jas 1:17).

There is an old hymn I learned growing up called "Count Your Blessings." It contains this refrain: "Count your blessings, name them one by one; Count your blessings, see what God hath done."[13] It says that as you count your blessings, "it will surprise you what the Lord hath done." Discontentment denies God's goodness. Thanksgiving and gratitude declare God's goodness.

Psalm 103 is a perfect example of counting your blessings. There is not one complaint in the entire psalm. It is an expression of unbridled joy in God for all that He has granted to us in His goodness. David, the author, exclaims, "Bless the Lord, O my soul; And all that is within me, bless His holy name! Bless the Lord, O my soul, And forget not all His benefits" (Ps 103:1–2). David goes on to count his blessings one by one, and in the end he is surprised at what the Lord has done. What are the blessings that he counts? God forgives my iniquities. He heals my diseases. He redeems my life from destruction. He feeds my mouth with good things. He renews my strength like an eagle's. After cataloguing these merciful gifts from God, it's no wonder David is so happy.

Paul's small but mighty exhortation in 1 Thessalonians will be a bulwark against discontentment: "in everything give thanks" (5:18). When God gives the believer a command, He also supplies him with the power to obey it. In any state or situation, you can achieve contentment as you choose to focus on what you have. Even in poverty you can give thanks that you have "every spiritual blessing in the heavenly places in Christ" (Eph 1:3).

I remember hearing a story of the farmer who learned contentment. He lived on the same farm all of his life. It was a fine farm, but after so many years the farmer wanted something different and something better. He started nit-picking and noticing all sorts of problems with the farm. Finally, he made the decision to sell the farm and contacted an agent. The agent wrote up a listing that showcased all of the farm's strengths: a great location, modern farm equipment, healthy livestock, and fertile soil. The agent read aloud the listing to the farmer for his final approval. Upon hearing what was written in the listing, the farmer said to the agent, "Stop everything. I changed my mind. I'm not going to sell this farm. I have been looking for a place like this my whole life!" Like the farmer came to learn, gratitude changes everything. Contentment comes not from getting everything you think you want but from wanting what you already have.

"Gratitude" comes from the same family of words as "grace," which means "unmerited favor." We have all received grace because we all started out as undeserving sinners. The only thing we earned or deserved on our own is wrath. Because of Christ's atoning sacrifice on the cross, God does not give us what our sins deserve but instead loves us in the Son (Ps 103:10–12; Eph 2:1–5). When we fully grasp what our sins deserved and the depths from which we've been saved, we will be awestruck by what we have been freely given in Christ. We will see that a God who already gave His Son to save us will not keep from us anything we need (Rom 8:32), and that realization will make our jaws drop. My friend, anything we receive short of hell is ground for great happiness. Are you looking for more than what God has mercifully given you in Christ?

I once read a book by Timothy Chester on pastor and theologian John Stott. The book is called *Stott on the Christian Life: Between Two Worlds*. In it he tells this insightful little story:

> Corey Widmer, one of his study assistants, would bring Stott coffee at 11:00 a.m. sharp each morning. With Stott deep in concentration, Widmer would quietly set the cup down on his desk. "I'm not worthy," Stott would mumble. At first Widmer found this amusing, but after a few months it started to bother him. Eventually he replied, "Oh, sure you are." At this, Stott stopped what he was doing and gave Widmer his undivided attention. "You haven't got your theology of grace right," he said with a combination of playfulness and earnestness. "It's only a cup of coffee," said Widmer defensively as he retreated from the room. "It's just the thin end of the wedge," Stott shouted after him as he left.[14]

Stott's point is this: Given who we are apart from Christ, given what we deserved, even a cup of coffee is a sign of God's goodness and mercy. It's an occasion for gratitude and thanksgiving. And, if we dare to move away from that perspective, it's the thin end of the wedge leading to ingratitude, arrogance, self-pity, and ultimately discontentment.

NURTURE LOVE

If you want to prevent covetousness from getting a hold of you, become a more loving person. Why do I say that? Because "love does not envy" (1 Cor 13:4). Let's work that out in simple terms. The more you covet, the less you love. The more you love, the less you covet. That seems to be the implication of this verse.

The word that Paul uses for "love" in 1 Corinthians 13 is the Greek *agapē*. It is the same word used for God's unconditional love for us in Christ. It is a word that Paul imbued with gospel meaning. It is a selfless, sacrificial love that seeks the highest good of others regardless of the cost to oneself, regardless of the unworthiness of the object. It was the ultimate display of *agapē* that Christ humbly came to earth to suffer and die on the cross for us (Rom 5:6–8; 1 Jn 4:7–11). That is our standard for love, and if we nurture this kind of love, it will extinguish covetousness. Covetousness wants to take from one's neighbor, while love desires the best for one's neighbor. They are opposing forces.

Let's compare the covetous spirit of King Saul with the sacrificial love of Saul's son Jonathan in 1 Samuel 18, which we referred to earlier. Remember Saul's reaction when he heard that David was receiving the greater praise? "Then Saul was very angry, and the saying displeased him; and he said, 'They have ascribed to David ten thousands, and to me they have ascribed only thousands. Now what more can he have but the kingdom?' So Saul eyed David from that day forward" (1 Sam 18:8–9). Stirred by jealousy and hatred, Saul attempted to kill David. Jonathan, however, loved David "as his own soul" (1 Sam 18:1). Jonathan's love for David was so strong that he risked his own life to protect and minister to his friend when he was being pursued by Saul in the wilderness (1 Sam 23:14–18). Be loving like Jonathan, not envious like Saul.

How can you foster *agapē* love for others? By making it your lifelong pursuit to understand God's unconditional love for you. When you linger near the cross and preach the gospel to yourself again and again, it stirs your heart to show others the love God has graciously shown you. Paul explains how this works: "For the love of Christ compels us, because we judge thus: that if One died for all, then all died; and He died for all, that those who live should live no longer for themselves, but for Him who died for them and rose again" (2 Cor 5:14–15). It's no wonder that Paul prays that we would "comprehend with all the saints what is the width and length and depth and height—to know the love of Christ which passes knowledge" (Eph 3:18–19). The more we grasp the magnitude of God's love, the more covetousness will be uprooted and replaced by an ever-growing desire to love, serve, and bless others for His glory.

TITHE,
AND THEN SOME

In Luke 12, a man approaches Jesus and says, "'Teacher, tell my brother to divide the inheritance with me'" (v. 13). The man is fixated on getting the money he thinks he deserves. He believes his only problem is that his brother is being greedy and unfair, but Jesus points out to him the greater problem: "'Take heed and beware of covetousness, for one's life does not consist in the abundance of the things he possesses'" (v. 15). The man's greed betrayed his covetous heart.

Pastor Kevin DeYoung explains how tightfistedness can be a symptom of greater sin:

> You might be coveting if you're unwilling to give up what you already have. Some people aren't interested in bigger and better. They just don't want to give up the safety and security of all they have. Again, the problem is not working hard, saving up, and being responsible with our assets. There are plenty of proverbs to commend this behavior. The problem is when we hold on tightly to our stuff instead of letting some of the blessings of prosperity slip through our fingers and fall to others.[15]

Going back to Luke 12, Jesus graciously proceeds to shepherd the man's heart through a parable. There was a rich farmer who had it all; his barns were full (vv. 16–20). It was time for the farmer to retire and enjoy his wealth—to eat, drink, and be happy. "Hold on a minute," God says. "You're being a fool. This is your last day on earth. Who will these riches belong to now?" Jesus concludes the story with a warning to the man who wants his brother's inheritance: "'So is he who lays up treasure for himself, and is not rich toward God'" (v. 21).

If hoarding and greed are symptoms of covetousness, giving and generosity are the cure. Herein lies the next principle for attaining contentment. Cultivate a generous spirit and practice giving to both God and neighbor. Exchange your getting with giving. The Bible teaches that giving is an antidote to covetousness.

Let's look once more at 1 Timothy 6. Paul warns Timothy about those who desire to be rich and the consequences of their greed. He says they "fall into temptation and a snare, and into many foolish and harmful lusts which drown men in destruction and perdition" (v. 9). Such men have "strayed from the faith . . . and pierced themselves through with many sorrows" (v. 10). It is frightening how discontentment and a lust for more can destroy your life and shipwreck your faith.

But Paul offers hope and a way out of the bondage. He says, "Command those who are rich in this present age not to be haughty, nor to trust in uncertain riches but in the living God, who gives us richly all things to enjoy" (1 Tim 6:17). The first step is to trust not in what you have or what you want but in God who provides all that you need. The next step is to give generously. Paul goes on to say, "Let them do good, that they be rich in good works, ready to give, willing to share, storing up for themselves a good foundation for the time to come, that they may lay hold on eternal life" (vv. 18–19). So, Paul says, in a sense, don't hoard riches here, but hoard riches in heaven! Seek to lay up treasures in heaven through serving and giving to His kingdom with your earthly wealth and strength. I've heard it said that if you want to be free from the love of money, then freely give your money to God's work and to the needy. God loves a cheerful giver (2 Cor 9:7)!

EMBRACE DIVINE PROVIDENCE

The providence of God is His sovereign rule over life and history. He ordains the affairs of man. He holds the planets in their orbit. He watches the sparrow as it falls. Providence is the ordering of life by God. Paul says that God works all things together after the counsel of His own will (Eph 1:11). He also says that God determines our times and the boundaries of nations, as "in Him we live and move and have our being" (Acts 17:26–28).

So, follow my logic. Your physical appearance, your family, your skills, your zip code, your lot in life, your financial situation, and every other fact about you are all a part of the tapestry of God's providence in your life. The God of the universe has decided who you are, what you look like, where you live, and what you have. That's the implication of providence.

Psalm 37:23 says, "The steps of a good man are ordered by the Lord, And He delights in his way." That is an important doctrine. God finds pleasure in His providence over your life, and you need to accept and embrace His providence if you are going to be content. If you do, it will help you live in the moment, whether easy or hard, with a settled peace that He has you where He wants you for good reason. It will help you deal with differences and conflicts with others.

Trusting His providence will free you to become your best self in Christ. You will value who you are without jealously comparing yourself to others. Because, the truth is, God broke the mold when He made you. Just as there are no two snowflakes the same, there are no two people the same. You were fearfully and wonderfully made by a masterful Creator (Ps 139:14). God knit you together in the womb with unique traits and abilities and brought you into a family, circumstance, and path that He ordained. As a believer, He gave you spiritual gifts through the Holy Spirit and assigned good works for you to do (1 Cor 12:1–11; Eph 2:10).

When you sincerely embrace providence, all that remains is to live out the one life He has given you to the best of your ability, for His glory. It is futile and frustrating to try to be someone else. Jesus makes this very point in the conversation with Peter we looked at earlier in the book (John 21:20–22). After hearing how he was going to die, Peter asked Christ about John's fate. But Jesus told Peter not to concern himself with that. Jesus said, "what is that to you? You follow Me'" (v. 22). Jesus taught Peter that his journey was different than John's. Living for Christ means minding your own business and being the best version of yourself for His glory. There is a work for Jesus that only you can do. So stop trying to be someone else, because if you are not yourself, this world is down a key player.

Let me illustrate how the doctrine of providence works out practically in our lives.[16] Amy Carmichael was born in 1867 in Northern Ireland, in a little seaside village called Millisle. I've been there many times. She grew up in a Christian home where her parents taught her the importance of loving and serving God. Amy was the oldest of seven children and often got her brothers and sisters into trouble with her youthful schemes.

As a child, Amy's favorite color was blue. She longed for beautiful blue eyes like her brother's and bemoaned the brown eyes God had given her. As her mother had instilled in her the truth that God answers prayer, she prayed every night that God would change her brown eyes to blue. To her dismay, every morning when she looked in the mirror, her eyes were still brown. Her mother pointed her to God's providence. Even though His answer to her prayer was "no," He must have given her brown eyes for a good reason.

You may know the rest of Amy Carmichael's story. God saved her and called her to be a missionary in India, where she established the Dohnavur Fellowship. Through her ministry, she rescued young girls from temple prostitution and enriched and enhanced the lives of many. What she came to understand later in life was that the Lord strategically gave her brown eyes. The Indian people identified with her because of them. They helped her to reach the lost with the love of Christ.

God knows what He is doing, even down to the color of your eyes. Accept who you are and the one life He has planned for you. Again, it doesn't mean you can't grow as a person or improve your situation. Contentment doesn't mean passivity, but it does mean living contentedly in the moment He has you in. Be able to say with King David, "O Lord, You are the portion of my inheritance and my cup; You maintain my lot. The lines have fallen to me in pleasant places; Yes, I have a good inheritance" (Ps 16:5–6).

PSALM 131:
PORTRAIT OF A QUIET SOUL

Calming yourself down when you are having a rough day or a rough season is easier said than done. It is a skill and discipline that few have mastered. Life more often than not has a way of winding us up, straining our nerves, and setting us on edge. That stress and distress can come from broken relationships, bad news from the doctor, financial hardships, failures on our part, dreams that haven't materialized, or the daily grind of waiting for something to change. How can we successfully handle those pressures with poise and peace of mind? In Psalm 131, King David shows us a glimpse into the heart of a person at rest, undisturbed and unperturbed by all the noise and nonsense going on around him. David is quiet on the inside, having learned the secret to gaining a peace that passes all understanding (Isa 26:3; Phil 4:7).

What can we learn from David? The first thing is to **accept our lot**. David emphatically declares that his heart is not haughty nor his eyes lofty (v. 1a). In other words, he understands his lowly position before God. He is convinced that God opposes the proud but gives grace to the humble (Ps 18:27; Ps 101:5; 1 Pet 5:5). Pride is a denial of dependence on God. David was not going to compete with God for control. He was accepting the lot that God had given him and not pining for what was outside of God's will. David's argument is that God blesses the life marked by humility and glad submission to God's will and ways (Micah 6:8). Serenity comes when we align our ambitions with God's will; we experience that the yoke of God's will is easy (Matt 11:28–29). Rest is found when we submit to God's wise providence, assured that it is His best for our benefit.

Second, David shows us the need to **accept our limits**. We must implicitly trust God with those things we cannot understand and that He does not explain (v. 1b). We are finite creatures under the hand of an infinite God. There are times when God's plans become inscrutable and His thoughts seem unreasonable. Times like that threaten to sap our energy, strain our faith, and disorient our thinking. That is when we need to follow David's lead. We shouldn't busy ourselves with problems we can't solve or questions we can't answer. We need to be still before God and leave those mysteries in His capable hands (Job 40:4; Ps 46:10). We will never know certain things, but we do know for certain the most important thing—that God works all things together for good for His saints (Rom 8:26–28).

Third, David teaches us by way of example to **accept our losses**. He says, "Surely I have calmed and quieted my soul, Like a weaned child with his mother" (v. 2). The process of weaning a baby from mother's milk to solid food is one of tussle and struggle. This battle of the wills was all the more fierce in Jewish culture because it took place when the child was bigger, between four and five years old. In this tug of war, the child is forced to give up the comfort of his mother's milk and learn contentment without it. He still craves milk, but mother knows what's best for him—solid food. In using this imagery, David admits that he had to surrender his own cherished ambitions to God and His ways. He came to understand that God is acting as a wise parent when He withholds or removes things from us. Maybe it is because we are too dependent on it and too independent from Him, or maybe He simply has something better in mind for us.

This quieting of the soul didn't come naturally or easily to David. He had to learn it through bitter experience. He gained self-mastery by God's grace. And, when he did, he experienced the peacefulness of a child at rest in his mother's arms, without a worry.

N

NIX UNGODLY DESIRES FOR MORE

D o you want to improve your life quite simply? Then apply this piece of wisdom: contentment comes not so much from great wealth as from fewer wants. The great English philosopher G. K. Chesterton said this: "There are two ways to get enough: one is to continue to accumulate more and more. The other is to desire less."[17] It's so simple but so good. Contentment is not a matter of addition but subtraction. Subtract ungodly desires and materialistic impulses for more, because when we seek things that don't please God and define life by the things we possess, they end up possessing us. We need to shrink our desires down to what our heavenly Father has lovingly chosen to provide for us at a given moment.

The author of Hebrews encourages this sort of subtraction. He says, "Let your conduct be without covetousness; be content with such things as you have. For He Himself has said, 'I will never leave you nor forsake you'" (Heb 13:5). Don't be characterized by a lust for more money and possessions, but be satisfied with what you have. Be grateful for what you've been given. Why? Because beyond the things you possess, you have God's presence and the promise that He will never leave you. In the Greek this promise is emphatic, conveying the impossibility of God ever deserting you. The promise is, literally, "I will never, never, never, never, not ever leave you." In this life, everything and everyone can be taken from you. And it will be taken from you in death. But, in life and death, nothing can separate you from God's presence and love (Rom 8:38–39). This is a certainty.

This truth is reinforced by Paul in 1 Timothy 6:6–8. He says that godliness accompanied by contentment is great gain—a blessed advantage—because we came into this world with nothing, and we will leave with nothing. Our material wealth in this life will be of no consequence in eternity. Paul goes on to say, however, that "having food and clothing, with these we shall be content" (v. 8). So, there is a place to base our contentment on what we have, but we need to shrink our expectations down to what He promises to provide (Luke 12:29–31; Phil 4:19). Do you have a roof over your head? Check. Some food in the cupboard? Check. A change of clothes in the wardrobe? Check. Then be content, because you are doing better than two-thirds of the world.

I love the less-is-more perspective we find in Proverbs. Listen to these words:

- *Better is a little with the fear of the Lord,*
  Than great treasure with trouble.
  Better is a dinner of herbs where love is,
  Than a fatted calf with hatred. (Prov 15:16–17)
- *Better is a little with righteousness,*
  Than vast revenues without justice. (Prov 16:8)

You need to look at your life and see the benefit of fewer things—as long as they are the right things. There are many people who may have more than you but more of the wrong things. Or, they have the right things with the wrong attitude. If you are living in the fear of the Lord, if you have righteousness through Christ, and if you have love, then you have the right things and the only necessary things. You don't need more; you just need to adjust your perspective.

Author Michael Moriarty articulately explains the virtue of living simply:

Simplicity as a conscious choice restores our equilibrium and illuminates our vision to see reality. Our inner resources are cleansed and our spiritual centers flourish when we resolve to live simple, uncomplicated lives. The late pioneer missionary Jim Elliot resolved: "The wisest life is the simple life. . . . Be on guard, my soul, of complicating your environment so that you have neither time nor room for growth."[18]

My mother was a simple woman. I greatly admired her for that. She had few wants. Sometimes when we would be out shopping with her at the mall, I would pick out something nice to buy for her. But, she would always say, "I don't need it." Then 10 minutes later she would say, "Don't you be buying me that!" She was perfectly content with the home she had lived in for 50 years. She had to be persuaded to buy anything for herself. If she did buy something, it was from the Goodwill or discount store, much to our chagrin. She loved to tell me about the treasures she found: a dress at a third of the price that had only been worn once or a Royal Doulton figurine for a few dollars. She kept those figurines in the china cabinet and would often tell the tale of how she discovered each treasure.

She was a simple, satisfied woman. After her passing, my daughters asked my father, "What was granny's favorite tea?" To which he replied, "Whatever tea was in the pot." That was the measure of her life. She was an incessant tea drinker, but her favorite flavor of tea was whatever-was-in-the-pot. I think her blue-collar upbringing had something to do with it. She lost her father to tuberculosis when she was only a little girl. She watched her bereaved mother go through hardship to provide for the family. As a child of the Second World War, she remembered living on rations and the preciousness of a block of butter or a pint of milk. I also think she was the way she was because she was a loving mother, happy to make sacrifices so that her children could have more.

But I think the main reason she was that way was because she loved the Lord, and He was sufficient for her. She had God, she had my father and his love, and she had children that loved God and followed Him. She had her King James Bible, and she had the little

Baptist church at the end of her street. She had enough and didn't desire more. The Lord was her Shepherd, so she did not want. As her son, I rise up to call her blessed (Prov 31:27–31). Her life and faith continue to minister to me, helping curb my instincts to complain or splurge unnecessarily. Her life is a call to get back to basics and be satisfied by the beauty of Jesus.

T

TAKE THE LONG VIEW

My friend, I encourage you to take the long view. Remembering this world is not our home and keeping an eternal perspective will help you find contentment and fight covetousness.

Paul says, "If then you were raised with Christ, seek those things which are above, where Christ is, sitting at the right hand of God. Set your mind on things above, not on things on the earth. For you died, and your life is hidden with Christ in God. When Christ who is our life appears, then you also will appear with Him in glory" (Col 3:1–4). Paul describes the heaven-mindedness that ought to characterize every believer. He is saying that if you've been saved by Christ unto new life, your thoughts should be fixed not on this life but on the next. You will have all that you want *then*. You will get to enjoy Christ in His full glory for eternity (Ps 16:11; 1 Pet 1:3–9). Delayed gratification is a Christian virtue, and having this mindset will help you stay focused. The Puritan pastor Richard Baxter said, "A heavenly mind is a joyful mind; this is the nearest and the truest way to live a life of comfort. . . . A heart in heaven will be a most excellent preservative against temptations, a powerful means to kill thy corruptions."[19]

Taking the long view means keeping the big picture of salvation at the forefront of our thoughts. We already have more than what we deserve because what we deserve is hell. Anything short of hell is reason to celebrate! So stop complaining. If we are saved, indwelt by the Holy

Spirit and living by the Word of God, then someday we will enter abundantly into the everlasting kingdom (2 Pet 1:11). What do we lack? What do we have to covet? What reason is there to envy others if we are so rich in Christ and have a glorious eternity with our King to look forward to (Matt 5:5; Eph 1:18)? The fact is, we as God's children are the ones to be envied. Unbelievers run after the things of the world and constantly come up short, never satisfied. But we possess and enjoy the satisfaction, peace, and hope that they crave. When you realize who you are in Christ, you will understand what an enviable position you are in.

An eternal perspective on possessions is a key to contentment. The world tells us that more stuff will make us happy. But the Bible says that all the material things we long for will be burned up along with this world (2 Pet 3:10–13). That is why Christ teaches: "'Do not lay up for yourselves treasures on earth, where moth and rust destroy and where thieves break in and steal; but lay up for yourselves treasures in heaven, where neither moth nor rust destroys and where thieves do not break in and steal'" (Matt 6:19–20). Heavenly treasures have no shelf life, no expiration date. Faith in the promise of eternal reward should compel us to spend our time, talent, and treasure investing in souls for eternity.

Eternity corrects and clarifies our perspective on the prosperity of the wicked. In Psalm 73, Asaph looked around him and saw the wicked prospering. Their lives were easy and smooth. Maybe he thought, "Boy, that's a nice house he's got, but I know how he got it. He's a gangster, profiting from wickedness. I'm keeping my hands clean, trying to be righteous, obeying the law, and they're wearing their arrogance and godlessness like a medallion. It bothers me. It makes me wonder, what's the point?" And then we read in verse 17, "Until I went into the sanctuary of God; Then I understood their end." Shifting his gaze to eternity snapped Asaph out of his envy and covetousness. He realized that there was a train coming down the track: the judgment of God. The tables will be turned. The wicked are going to be punished, and the righteous are going to be rewarded. Asaph regains his footing, finding contentment and peace in his all-sufficient God. He says, "Whom have I in heaven but You? And there is none upon earth that I desire besides You. My flesh and my heart fail; But God is the strength of my heart and my portion forever" (vv. 25–26).

It reminds me of the story of the Morrisons, who were missionaries to Africa. After a life of sacrificial service for the gospel, Henry Morrison and his wife had hardly any money to retire on, and their health was broken. They were defeated and discouraged. Many of their friends had left them over time, and the churches that had supported them had abandoned them. On the ship back home to New York from Africa, they discovered that they were fellow passengers with President Teddy Roosevelt, who had been in Africa on a big-game hunting expedition. They envied the fuss everyone was making over the president. They thought, "Here are we, living lives of faithful service to God, and no one cares about us."

The feelings grew worse when their ship docked in New York and they saw the crowds and fanfare welcoming the president home. They got off the ship and slipped away to their meager lodgings in a quiet part of the city. Henry felt downright depressed and deflated. He said, "I can't take this." His wife replied, "You know what? You need to talk to the Lord." Henry disappeared and then emerged some hours later in a better state of mind. He told his wife, "The Lord settled it with me. I told him how bitter I was that the president should receive this tremendous homecoming when no one welcomed us home after so many years of faithfulness. And, when I finished, it seemed as though the Lord put His hand on my shoulder and simply said, 'But you are not home yet.'"[20]

That is the right perspective. It is a constant gaze toward heaven that brings contentment in the midst of meagerness and longing for what others have. We are not home yet. The meek will inherit the earth (Matt 5:5). Just wait a little while longer. We are going to enter into His everlasting kingdom abundantly. Christ is going to welcome us home with these comforting words: "'Well done, good and faithful servant. . . . Enter into the joy of your lord'" (Matt 25:23).

I have heard it said that life is not about waiting for the storm to pass, but it is about learning to dance in the rain. Learning contentment is a way to learn to dance in the rain. Therefore, I pray that this little booklet will help you run from covetousness and chase contentment until it is happily found in our sufficient Savior, Jesus Christ.

ACKNOWLEDGEMENTS

Life is a team sport and writing a book is a collaborative effort. There are several sets of fingerprints over the pages of this booklet. To the leaders and members of Kindred Community Church—thank you for your love, commitment, and faithful support. Thank you for letting me pursue ministry with great joy.

To the Know The Truth board, volunteers, and office staff—much appreciation for your time, talents, and treasure. Special thanks to Todd Elliott, Jerry Motto, Danielle Bracey, Estella Roach, Phil Siefert, Kara Bray, and Beth De Courcy.

I also want to single out Joan Shim for her invaluable assistance in penning this booklet and Briana Sukert for her editing input.

Finally, I continue to be deeply indebted to my wife, June, and family for their encouragement and enrichment in life and ministry.

It has been well said that a contented mind is a continual feast, and so I pray that those who purchase this book will become satisfied customers in Christ's all-sufficiency.

Philip De Courcy
Anaheim Hills, CA

ENDNOTES

FLEEING DISCONTENTMENT

1 Gary Inrig, *True North: Discovering God's Way in a Changing World* (Grand Rapids, MI: Discovery House, 2002), 104.

2 Jeremiah Burroughs, *The Rare Jewel of Christian Contentment* (Mulberry, IN: Sovereign Grace Publishers, Inc., 2001), 1.

3 C.S. Lewis, *The Weight of Glory* (New York: HarperOne, 2001), 26.

FINDING CONTENTMENT

4 This poem was written by Jason Lehman and found in a message by Dr. Charles R. Swindoll entitled "Who Gets the Glory?", preached at Northwest Bible Church in Dallas, TX.

5 J.C. Ryle, *Thoughts for Young Men* (Carlisle, PA: The Banner of Truth Trust, 2015), 21.

6 Thomas Watson, *The Art of Divine Contentment* (United Kingdom, n.p., 1829), 174.

7 Ibid., 177.

8   Ibid., 181.

9   Warren Wiersbe, *The Bumps Are What You Climb On: Encouragement for Difficult Days* (Grand Rapids, MI: BakerBooks, 2016), 155.

10   Paul W. Powell, *A Faith that Sings* (Nashville, TN: B&H Publishing Group, 1991), 53.

11   Wiersbe, 155.

12   Arnell Motz, pastor of International Evangelical Church; Addis Ababa, Ethiopia; source: *The Province* of Vancouver, British Columbia (9-19-90)

13   Johnson Oatman Jr., "Count Your Blessings." Hymnal.net: https://www.hymnal.net/en/hymn/h/707

14   Tim Chester, *Stott on the Christian Life: Between Two Worlds* (Wheaton, IL: Crossway, 2020), 230.

15   Kevin DeYoung, *The Ten Commandments: What They Mean, Why They Matter, and Why We Should Obey Them* (Wheaton, IL: Crossway, 2018), 163–164.

16   Missionaries of the World, "Amy Wilsom Carmichael." Posted June 19, 2011. Missionaries of the World: https://www.missionariesoftheworld.org/2011/06/amy-wilson-carmichael_8197.html

17   Source unknown.

18   Michael G. Moriarty, *The Perfect 10: The Blessings of Following God's Commandments in a Postmodern World* (Grand Rapids, MI: Zondervan, 1999), 221.

19   Richard Baxter, *The Saints' Everlasting Rest,* new edition edited by William Young (Philadelphia: J.B. Lippincott Co., 1909), 252, 257.

20   Doug McIntosh, *Life's Greatest Journey* (Chicago: Moody Press, 2000), 228–229.

In a world where people are never satisfied and always clamoring for more, discontentment can easily creep into our hearts and lives. And while it may seem like a small thing, it can be a gateway to covetousness, envy, and other sins that dishonor God and leave you feeling miserable. That is why a proactive pursuit of contentment is essential for the healthy Christian.

In his new book, *Contentment Spelled Out*, Pastor Philip De Courcy highlights the dangers of dissatisfaction and sets before us a practical path to attaining a lasting biblical contentment that is rooted in Christ, His character, and His promises. As you understand and apply the principles in this book, you too can learn, along with the Apostle Paul, the secret of being content in any situation.

Pastor and author Philip De Courcy is the teacher on Know The Truth, a media ministry whose passion and purpose is to acclaim and proclaim God's eternal truth as found in Holy Scriptures. Pastor Philip's messages originate from his weekly Bible teaching at Kindred Community Church and are centered upon the person and work of Jesus Christ, God's Son. The ministry of Know The Truth is shared daily on the radio, website (KTT.org), digital media platforms, and in print, boldly proclaiming the truth that all can be set free to enjoy God fully and forever through the work of Jesus Christ.

f /kttradio ⓘ /philipdecourcy 🐦 /philipdecourcy
P.O. Box 30250, Anaheim, CA 92809
888-644-8811 • KTT.org

$7.99
ISBN 978-1-7360801-2-2
50799>

9 781736 080122